Ginn Mathematics

TEXTBOOK 1

Rose Griffiths

GINN

Contents

Before you start...

Some notes about using this book

Working with a friend

You can do most of the activities in this book on your own, but it is better to work with a friend, if possible.

Talk to your friend about your work, and explain to each other how you got your answers.

Using equipment

Use the equipment suggested on the pages, to help you do each activity. Sometimes you might think of other equipment which could help you, too.

Don't forget to tidy up after yourself!

Answers

Ask your teacher for the Answers Booklet from the Teachers' Resource Book if you are marking your work yourself.

If you do not understand something, always ask your teacher to discuss it with you.

Count in twos.
How many slippers are there?
2, 4, 6, 8. There are 8.

I can work it out on a calculator, too.

2 in
each pair | 4
pairs | | 4
pairs | 2 in
each pair

2 x 4 = **or** 4 x 2 =

Try it yourself.

1 How many boots are here?

2 Copy and complete:

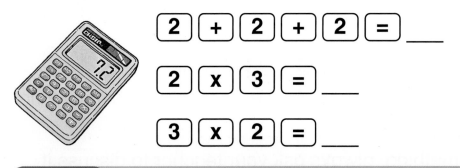

2 + 2 + 2 = ___

2 x 3 = ___

3 x 2 = ___

Count in twos ...

How many trainers are there?

How many mittens are there?

How many gloves are there?

How many socks are there?

Copy and complete :

Twos	
0 x 2 = _____	2 x 0 = _____
1 x 2 = _____	2 x 1 = _____
2 x 2 = _____	2 x 2 = _____
3 x 2 = _____	2 x 3 = _____
4 x 2 = _____	2 x 4 = _____
5 x 2 = _____	2 x 5 = _____

You need a real clock to do these pages.

Make your clock show 4 o'clock to start with.

Watch the hands move.
Make your clock show these times:

1
A quarter past
four

2
Half past
four

3
A quarter to
five

4 When you changed the time,
   did **both** the hands move, or just the big hand?

5 Turn the hands on your clock
   to show **five o'clock.**

   Draw it in your book.

Turn the hands on your clock to show these times.
Write down the times.

7   8   9

A quarter past
_____

?   ?   ?

Turn the hands on your clock
to show **a quarter past six.**

Draw it in your book.

This is the time
when my brother
went to bed.

Write down the time.

This is when I went to bed.
Write down the time.

Number collection

Kate and Jack have made
a number collection.
You could make one too.
Work with a friend, if you can.

Draw pictures to show
where you have seen numbers.

Make a poster, a book or a display
to show the numbers you find.

ind different ways
f making each number.

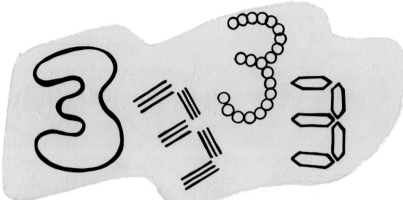

Can you say each
number out loud?
Check with a friend.

It costs six
hundred and
ninety five pounds.

What does each number
ell you?

This number tells me
which page I'm on
in my reading book.

alk about the numbers in your collection
ith your friends.

How much money is this?

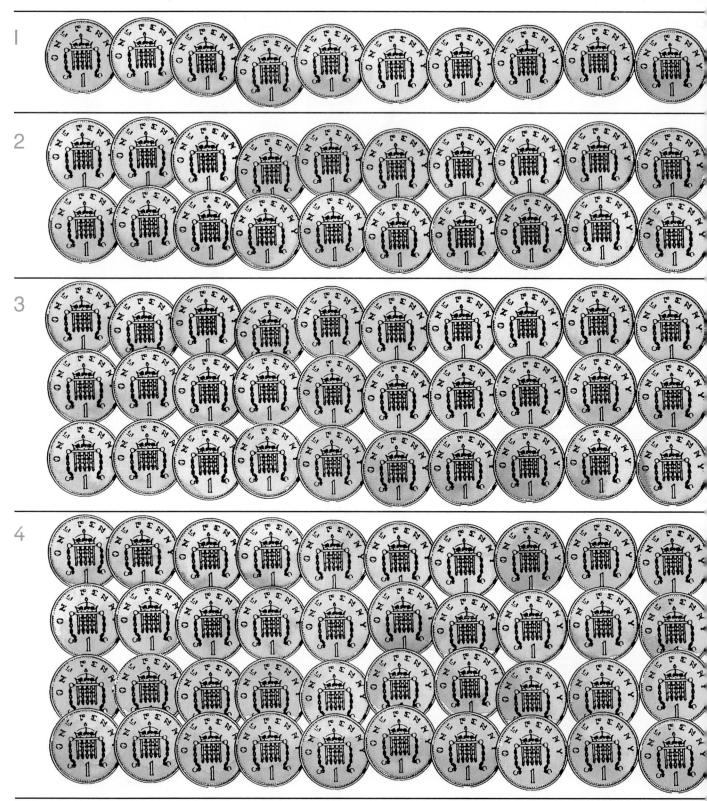

1

2

3

4

5 How much money is there on this page altogether?

Find out more about ways of making £1 ...

You could use :

some coins, paper and pencil, coin rubber stamps and an ink pad.

You need 100 pennies to make £1.

How many 50p pieces make £1?

How many 2p pieces do you need to make £1?

How many 5p pieces do you need to make £1?

How many 10p pieces make £1?

10 What about 20p pieces?

Snail trails

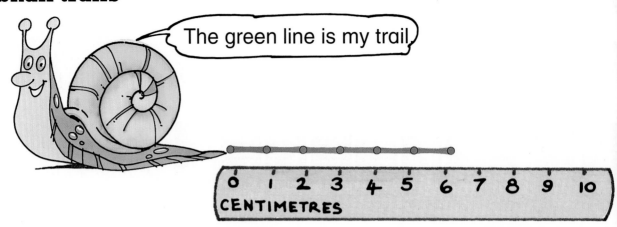

The green snail's trail measures 6 cm.

This trail measures 9 cm.

Measure these trails.

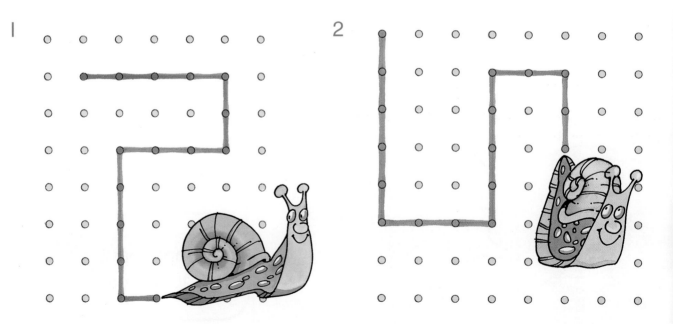

1

2

Measure these trails.

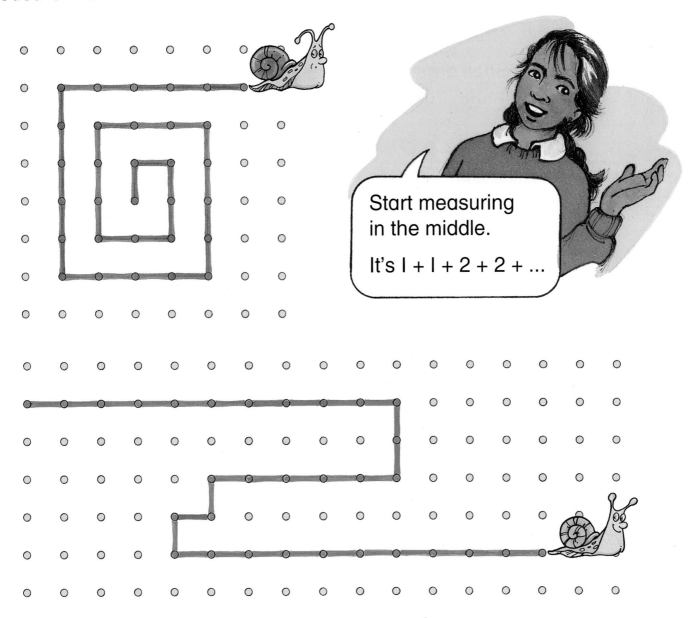

Start measuring in the middle.

It's 1 + 1 + 2 + 2 + ...

Use some spotty paper.
Draw a snail trail which measures
more than 100 cm.

You can ask a friend
to check it!

More snail trails

Red Snail and Blue Snail always start and finish together, when they make trails.

Red Snail turns just once. She goes

Blue Snail likes turning! She goes

| Look at these trails.

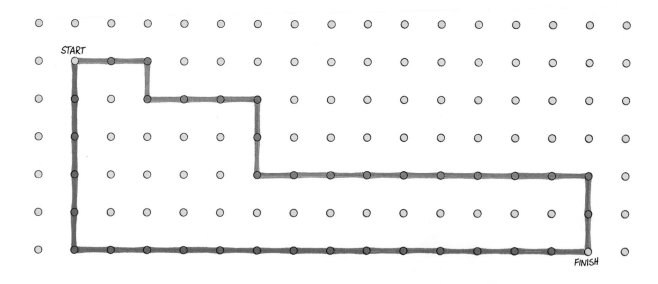

(a) What does Red Snail's trail measure?

(b) What does Blue Snail's trail measure?

Measure these trails.

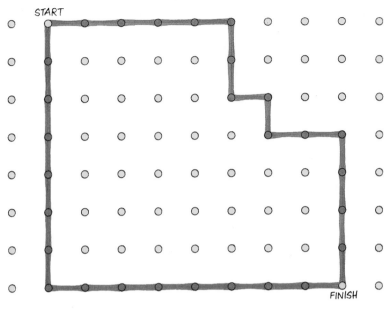

START

FINISH

You could
write your answers
like this:

2 Red Snail's trail
7 + 8 = 15
15 cm

Blue Snail's trail
5 + 2 + 1 + ...

Measure these trails.
Is Red Snail's trail shorter than Blue's?

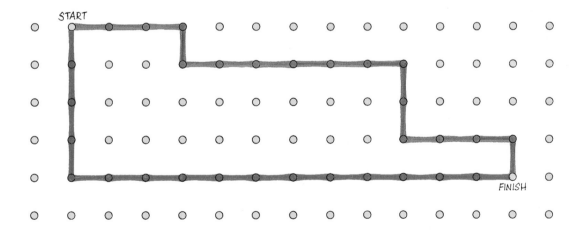

START

FINISH

Use some spotty paper.
Draw some more trails for Red Snail and
Blue Snail, like the ones on this page.
Measure them. What do you notice?

Clocks and watches

Digital watches and clocks show the time like this ...

This watch says six fifteen. That's a quarter past six.

| Copy this chart. (You could use a rubber stamp for the clocks.) Draw the hands on the clocks.

	What time is it?	
6:30	Six thirty. Half past six.	
6:45	Six forty five. Quarter to seven.	
7:00	Seven o'clock.	
7:15	Seven fifteen. Quarter past seven.	

It will be lunchtime at 12 o'clock.

This is the school clock at twelve o'clock.

This is my watch at twelve o'clock.

We'll play football at half past twelve.

Draw the school clock.

3

We'll go swimming at a quarter past two.

Draw my watch.

We'll have a story at a quarter to three.

Draw my watch.

5

We'll all go home at a quarter past three.

Draw the school clock.

You need:
£1 in pennies (real pennies are best!)
£1 in ten pences.

1 Count the pennies to make sure you have £1.

2 Count the ten pences to make sure you have £1.

3 Which is quicker to count,

£1 in ten pences **or** £1 in pennies?

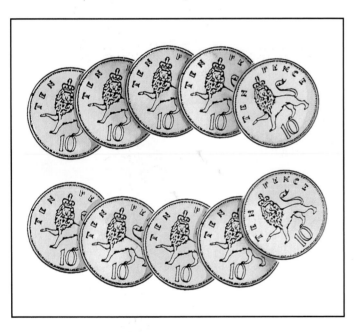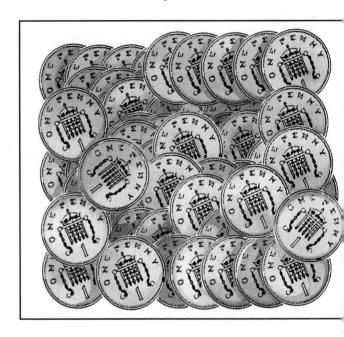

We can put things in tens to make them easier to count.

se the money to do some sums,
ke this :

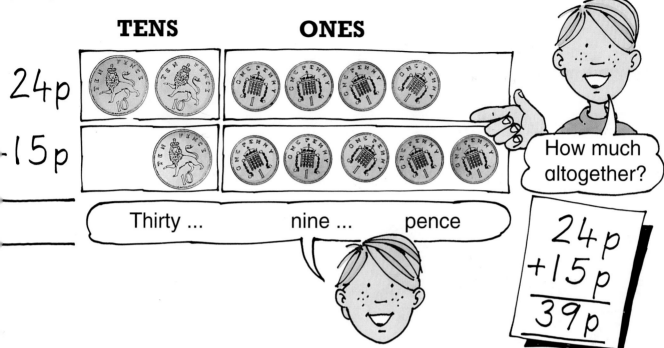

TENS   ONES

24p

-15p

Thirty ...   nine ...   pence

How much
altogether?

24p
+15p
───
39p

se money to do these.

```
    42p          5      60p          6      14p
   +21p                +11p                +32p
   ─────                ─────                ─────
```

```
    56p          8      32p          9      45p
   +23p                +62p                +13p
   ─────                ─────                ─────
```

```
    24p
   +16p
   ─────
```

Hint
You can swap
ten pennies
for a ten pence.

Threes

Join some multilink
(or other cubes)
together in 3s.

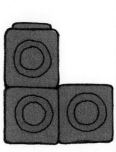

I **How many cubes?**

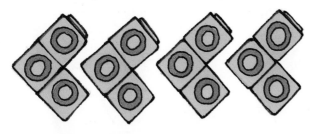

(a) 3 + 3 + 3 + 3 = _____

(b) 4 threes = _____

2

You can do this
on a calculator, too.

Try adding : ⬚3 ⬚+ ⬚3 ⬚+ ⬚3 ⬚+ ⬚3 ⬚= __

or multiplying : ⬚4 ⬚x ⬚3 ⬚= __

---

3 **How many cubes?**

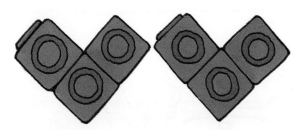

(a) 3 + 3 = _____

(b) 2 threes = _____

(c) ⬚3 ⬚+ ⬚3 ⬚= __

(d) ⬚2 ⬚x ⬚3 ⬚= __

How many cubes?

(a) 3 + 3 + 3 + 3 + 3 = _____

(b) 5 threes = _____

(c) [5] [x] [3] [=] ___

How many cubes?

NONE!

(a) No threes = _____

(b) [0] [x] [3] [=] ___

How many cubes?

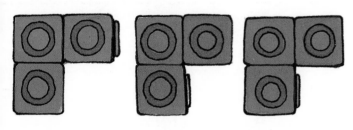

(a) 3 + 3 + 3 = _____

(b) 3 threes = _____

(c) [3] [x] [3] [=] ___

I've got 18 cubes.
How many 3s can I make?

Shape names

Use this page to help you with the questions on the next few pages.

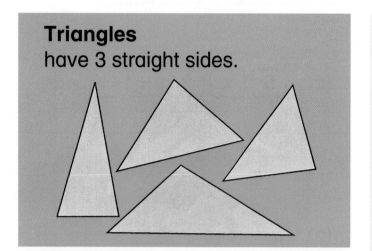

Triangles
have 3 straight sides.

Quadrilaterals
have 4 straight sides.

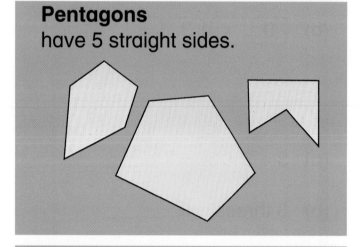

Pentagons
have 5 straight sides.

Rectangles
have 4 straight sides
and 4 right-angles.

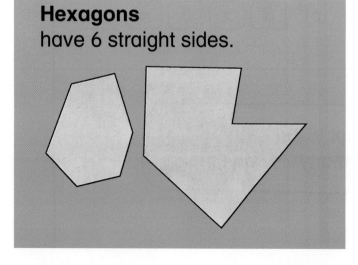

Hexagons
have 6 straight sides.

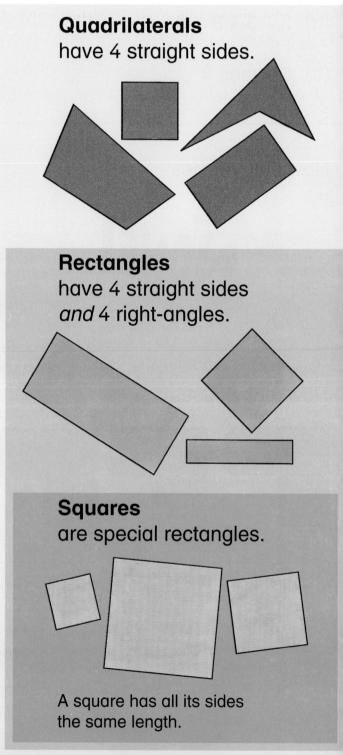

Squares
are special rectangles.

A square has all its sides
the same length.

What are the names of these shapes?

Count the sides and name each shape.

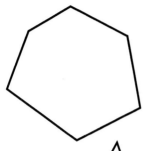

2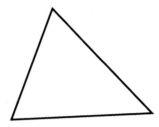

3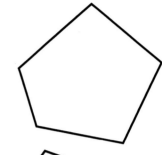

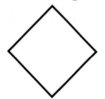

5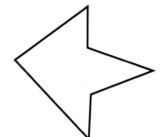

6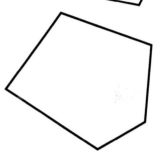

Write **Yes** or **No** for these :

Is this a square?

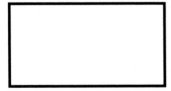

8 Is this a triangle?

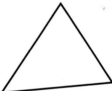

Is this a rectangle?

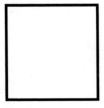

10 Is this a quadrilateral?

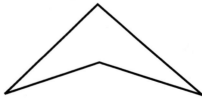

Is this a square?

12 Make up some more questions like these. Try them on a friend.

Dotty patterns

I've drawn some patterns on spotty paper.

I drew squares to make this pattern :

What shapes did I use for these?

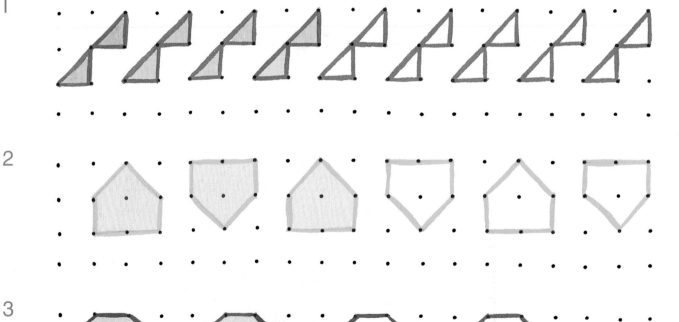

1

2

3

Use spotty paper.

Copy some of these patterns.
Make up some patterns
of your own.

Write down the
shapes you can see
in your patterns.

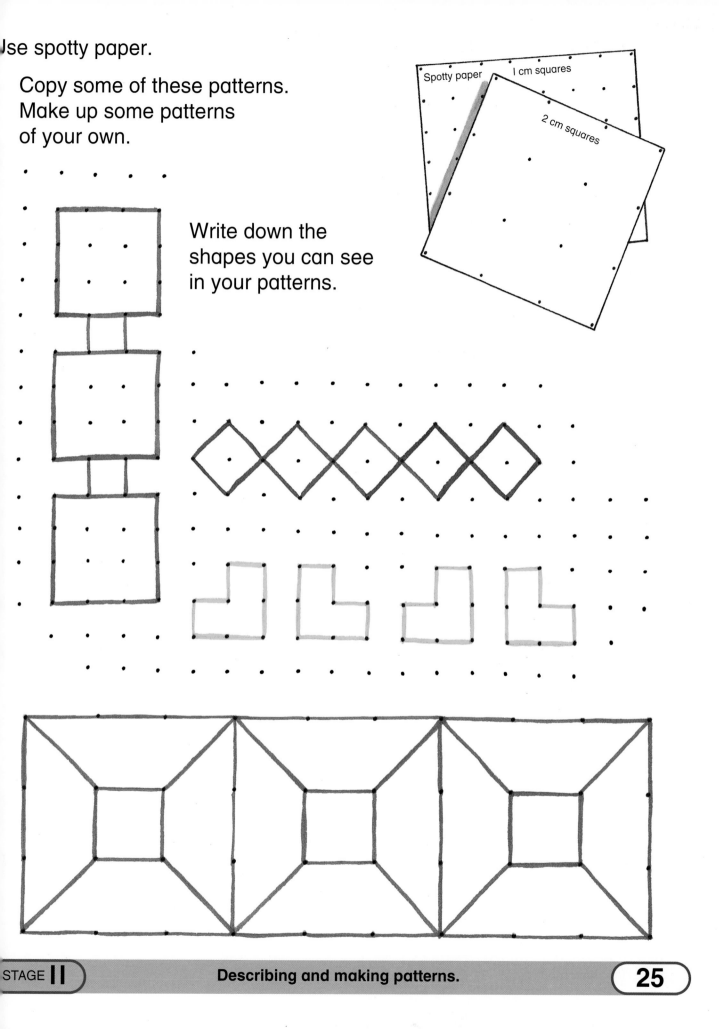

Coins for snacks

There is a snack machine at our swimming pool.

You have to put in the right money.

I want to buy some cheese biscuits. They cost 35p.

1 Can I pay for my biscuits like this?

2 Can I pay for my biscuits like this?

3 How many ways can you make 35p, if you can only use 20p, 10p and 5p coins?

Draw or print all the different ways you can find. How many ways are there?

PS The order of the coins does not matter

counts as the **same a**

What comes next?

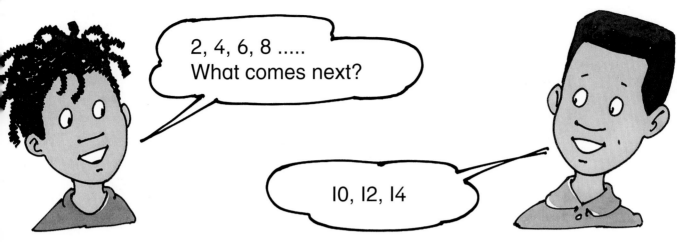

opy these.
Write down the next three numbers, as well.

5, 10, 15, 20, ...

62, 63, 64, 65, ...

90, 80, 70, 60, ...

22, 24, 26, 28, ...

5

95, 96, 97, 98, ...

22, 20, 18, ...

65, 60, 55, ...

10, 20, 30, ...

9 Can you count
up to 100.....
in twos?
in fives?
in tens?

Ask a friend
to listen to you.

Breakfast

I've drawn a chart.
It shows what I had for
breakfast this week.

I always have toast.

Sometimes I have jam on it :

Sometimes I have peanut butter :

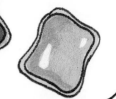

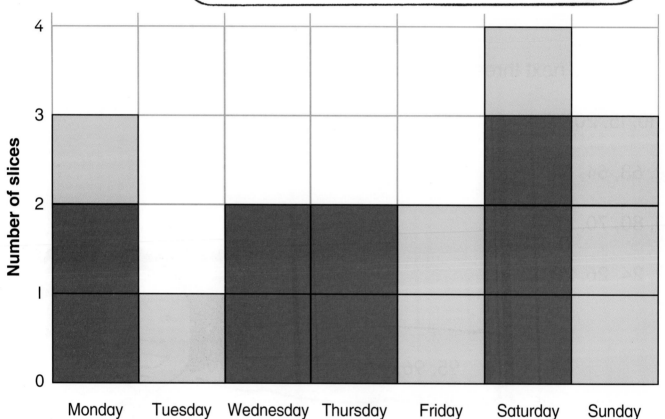

On Monday I had
2 slices with jam and
I slice with peanut butter.

Do **you** like
peanut butter?

What is your favourite jam?

What did I eat for breakfast
on Wednesday?

What did I eat on Friday?

5 Which day did I have
   3 slices of toast
   with peanut butter?

6 How many slices of toast
   with peanut butter did I eat
   altogether this week?

How many slices of toast with jam
did I eat altogether this week?

Which day was I **very** hungry
when I woke up?

Change from £1

You could use:

some coins, coin rubber stamps and an ink pad.

This cost me
45p.
I paid with £l.

I got 55p change.

This is one way of making 55p.

I can check my change is right,
like this:

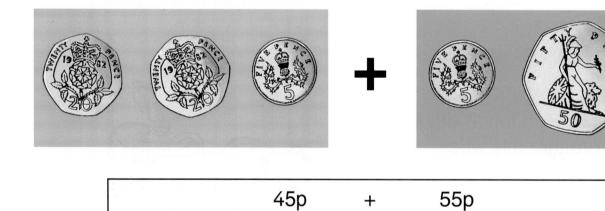

45p	+	55p

Does this add up to £l?

Yes, so my change **is** right.

raw or print coins to show
he way of giving change to each person.

eck the change by adding up.

2

This cost me
60p.
I paid with £I.

This cost me
85p.
I paid with £I.

4

This cost me
35p.
I paid with £I.

This pack of pens
cost me 72p.
I paid with £I.

Make up a problem like these
for one of your friends to do.

Mirror pictures

You need a mirror
for this page.

Put the mirror on each picture, on the dotted line,
to make each animal complete.

Draw half a picture yourself, like these.
Look at it with a mirror.

Draw some more half pictures if you want to.